You can Save the Planet

The Great Outdoors: Saving Habitats

Richard Spilsbury

Heinemann
LIBRARY

H www.heinemann.co.uk/library

Visit our website to find out more information about Heinemann Library books.

To order:
- ☎ Phone 44 (0) 1865 888066
- 📄 Send a fax to 44 (0) 1865 314091
- 💻 Visit the Heinemann Bookshop at www.heinemann.co.uk/library to browse our catalogue and order online.

First published in Great Britain by Heinemann Library, Halley Court, Jordan Hill, Oxford OX2 8EJ, part of Harcourt Education. Heinemann is a registered trademark of Harcourt Education Ltd.

© Harcourt Education Ltd 2005
First published in paperback in 2006
The moral right of the proprietor has been asserted.

Editorial: Nancy Dickmann and Dave Harris
Design: Richard Parker and Q2A Solutions
Illustrations: Q2A and Jeff Edwards
Picture Research: Maria Joannou and Virginia Stroud-Lewis
Production: Camilla Smith

Originated by Dot Gradations Limited
Printed in China by WKT Company Limited

ISBN-10:   0 431 04172 4 (hardback)
ISBN-13: 978 0 431 04172 8 (hardback)
09 08 07 06 05
10 9 8 7 6 5 4 3 2 1

ISBN-10:   0 431 04178 4 (paperback)
ISBN-13: 978 0 431 04178 0 (paperback)
10 09 08 07 06
10 9 8 7 6 5 4 3 2 1

British Library Cataloguing in Publication Data

Spilsbury, Richard
The Great Outdoors: Saving Habitats.
– (You Can Save the Planet)
333.9'516
A full catalogue record for this book is available from the British Library.

Acknowledgements

The publishers would like to thank the following for permission to reproduce photographs: Alamy/Elmtree Images p. **11**; Alamy/Philip Lewis p. **12**; Alamy/Piper Lehman p. **5**; Ardea/John Cancalosi p. **17**; Auscape p. **22**; Corbis/Niall Benvie p. **25**; Corbis/B. Borrell Casals, Frank Lane Picture Agency p. **20**; Corbis/Gary Braasch pp. **10**, **26**; Corbis/Josef Polleross p. **14**; Corbis/Reuters pp. **21**, **24**; Corbis/Roy Corral p. **7**; FLPA/Minden p. **15**; Getty Images p. **16**; Getty Images/Photodisc pp. **4**, **19**; ICCE/Howard Morland pp. **8**, **18**; NHPA/Kitchin V Hurst p. **9**; NHPA/Stephen Dalton p. **27**; NHPA/Hellio Van Ingen p. **23**; Yell Limited p. **13**.

Cover photograph of a family hiking, reproduced with permission of Corbis/Tom Stewart.

The publishers would like to thank Nick Lapthorn of the Field Studies Council for his assistance in the preparation of this book.

Every effort has been made to contact copyright holders of any material reproduced in this book. Any omissions will be rectified in subsequent printings if notice is given to the publishers.

The paper used to print this book comes from sustainable resources.

Contents

Words appearing in the text in bold, **like this**, are explained in the Glossary.

What are habitats?

Habitats are places where wildlife lives. Some of these habitats are wild places, far from where people live, such as deep oceans and remote deserts. There are also more familiar habitats you may have visited on days out or holidays, such as woodlands, hills, beaches, lakes, and rivers. There are even human-made habitats, such as gardens, dotted amongst the buildings in the towns and cities where most of us live.

People can get close to wildlife in this pond habitat.

Sadly, many habitats have already been badly disturbed or even destroyed by people. The wildlife that lives there may then have nowhere else to live. This book is about how you can make a difference and help to save some of the planet's habitats, both natural and human-made!

How do habitats work?

The place where a living thing spends its life is called a habitat. A habitat provides animals and plants with what they need to survive. Every living thing needs water to drink, food to eat, and shelter from danger. Habitats can be big or small. A large animal such as a grizzly bear might spend its life roaming far and wide across a forest habitat. A tiny insect might spend its whole life on a single leaf. Some wild places contain a variety of different habitats. At a coast, for example, some animals live in rock pools, others in the sand, and some on the cliffs.

There may be lots of different types of animals and plants living in each habitat. Together they form an **ecosystem**. Each ecosystem in the world is different, with a different mix of living things. However, ecosystems can be grouped into different types such as lakes, rivers, or woodlands.

Habitat + different living things that live there = ecosystem!

Science Behind It: Food chains and webs

Food chains and **food webs** are diagrams that help explain what ecosystems are like. They show the living things in a habitat that eat each other to get energy. All living things need energy to live. Green plants trap the Sun's energy to make their own food. Animals get this energy when they eat plants, or by eating other animals that eat plants. Each living thing is a link in an energy chain. For instance, in a field the first link might be grass, the next a rabbit that eats grass, and the next a fox that eats rabbits. The last link in this chain is a **decomposer** such as **bacteria**, which help break down the fox's body after it has died. This releases **nutrients** into the soil that grass uses to grow. Food webs show how different food chains are joined together.

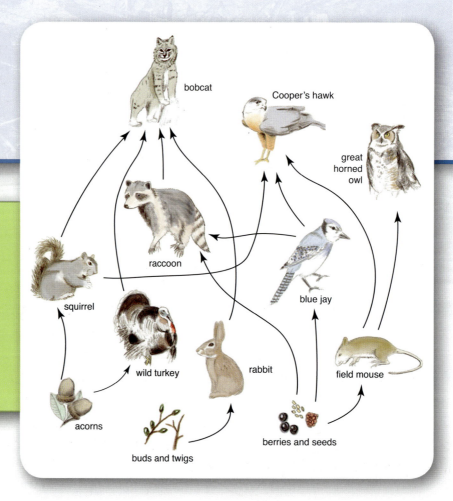

This food web shows some of the plants and animals that live in a forest, and what they eat.

bobcat

Cooper's hawk

great horned owl

raccoon

squirrel

blue jay

wild turkey

rabbit

field mouse

acorns

buds and twigs

berries and seeds

The living things in a habitat rely on each other in different ways. For example, bees need the nectar (sugary liquid) and rich **pollen** in flowers to feed themselves and their families. Plants rely on visiting bees to carry pollen into their flowers so they can make seeds.

This caribou lives in a habitat with many other plants and animals.

Taking Action: Know your habitats

Try to make a simple map of the habitats, both natural and human-made, in and around where you live. You could choose your school grounds or the neighbourhood around your home. Imagine what the area looks like from above. Take a good look around and mark on your map where different habitats are. These might be woodland, fields, gardens, and hedges. You might be surprised at how many different types of wild places there are!

Why are habitats under threat?

Habitats, especially wild ones, face many threats. Some are natural dangers, such as strong winds that blow down trees or high waves that wash away beaches or flood the land. There is not much we can do about these problems. But the biggest threats by far come from people.

When people dug out the ground to build this quarry they destroyed the habitats of many animals.

Habitat destruction

People are destroying or changing habitats all over the Earth. Miners dig enormous holes in hills and deserts to search for oil, coal, rocks, and gemstones. Foresters cut down ancient forests to sell or burn the wood. They sell the clear land for growing crops, or building houses and roads. Factories dump their poisonous and **polluting** waste into the oceans and rivers of the world. Cars, planes, and other vehicles produce gases that pollute the air all around us.

Ruining ecosystems

Living things are **adapted** to their particular habitat. When people destroy or change habitats the animals that lived there are forced to move out. Many animals are unable to survive because there is nowhere else for them to go, or they cannot find the food they need in a new habitat.

Hundreds of **species** of plants and animals have become **extinct** because of people. We hunt millions of wild animals each year, such as kangaroos and sharks. We catch too many fish from whole areas of ocean. Sometimes the animals that we bring with us into new habitats, such as cats and goats, kill the wild animals and plants that already live there.

Raccoons are wild animals that can adapt to different habitats, from forests to backyards. This raccoon is searching for leftover food in a waste bin.

Why save wild places?

We need to save wild places for lots of reasons. They are fascinating places to visit and learn about wildlife. If a habitat is destroyed or a species becomes extinct it can never be replaced. Wild places are vital for the survival of all living things. Everything in an **ecosystem**, including people, is connected. When we damage wild places we also put ourselves in danger.

Taking Action: Make a difference

Some of the problems facing habitats may seem too big for you to do anything about. But we can all make a difference. You can help faraway wild places by joining an organization such as WWF, Friends of the Earth, or Greenpeace. For ideas on how to help habitats closer to home, check out the other Taking Action boxes in this book.

Trees make **oxygen** that living things need to breathe. When people cut down trees there is less clean air for all of us.

How can we look after woodlands and forests?

Woodlands and forests are home to lots of wildlife, from woodpeckers and wood ants to wolves. These **habitats** need our help! All over the world many thousands of square kilometres of trees are being chopped down each week. People cut down trees to make space for things such as farms, factories, airports, and rubbish dumps. Trees are also cut down to make many products, including paper and furniture.

Sometimes forests are cleared to make space for new towns. By making habitats for ourselves, we can destroy habitats for wild animals and plants.

How can we help?

There are many ways you can help to save woodlands. Whenever possible, use less paper and buy **recycled** paper products. Trees do not need to be chopped down to make recycled paper. Recycled paper is made from paper and cardboard that has already been used.

When you are out and about

Help woodlands and forests when you are out by taking care not to damage trees. Never break tree branches or carve initials into tree bark. Both of these things can injure a living tree. Do not collect firewood from wild woods because old wood is a vital part of the **ecosystem**. It provides shelter and food for many small animals. As it rots, **nutrients** from the wood drain into the soil and nourish the growth of new trees.

Taking Action: Stop forest fires

Fires can spread quickly through dry trees and cause terrible damage. People cause many forest fires. You can help by learning these fire-safety rules.

- Clear plants and leaves away from a camp fire before lighting it.
- Throw soil, sand, or water on your fire to put it out or to keep it from getting too big.
- Always make sure a fire is out before you leave it.
- Never use fireworks or drop matches in wild places.

Fires that are under safe control can be fun. You can help to prevent forest fires by following the fire-safety rules.

Case Study: Protecting trees with telephone directories!

In the UK, schoolchildren help to plant trees and protect woodlands by **recycling** old telephone directories!

In the Yellow Woods Challenge, schools compete for prizes by collecting as many old *Yellow Pages* telephone directories as possible. Some schools also enter a competition to build giant sculptures from them. All the directories are then taken away and recycled instead of being thrown away. Recycling directories is a much better idea because they can be made into all kinds of new things such as egg boxes, art paper, newspaper, padded envelopes, and cardboard.

The makers of *Yellow Pages* also help a **conservation** group called the Woodland Trust. They give money to the Woodland Trust to help it plant and protect trees all over the UK.

In the Yellow Woods Challenge, schoolchildren can also win prizes by making sculptures out of the directories they have collected before they are recycled.

How can we help protect mountains and hills?

Mountains and hills may look quiet or bare, but they are home to a variety of wildlife. Among the trees on the lower slopes, there are woodland animals such as squirrels and bears. In the grasses and shrubs higher up the mountain live animals such as rabbits and foxes. At the rocky mountain-tops, insects crawl among the scattered plants and eagles nest in the craggy cliffs.

These plastic drink bottles were left by tourists on Mount Sinai in Egypt.

What problems do mountains face?

People damage mountain and hill **habitats** in different ways. Lots of people visit mountains to walk or ski. This means that local people earn money from **tourism**, but the habitat can suffer. Large numbers of tourists erode (wear away) paths, trample plants, and leave litter. This litter **pollutes** the land and can harm animals. Pet dogs can disturb nesting birds and other wildlife.

Other threats

People cut down the forests that grow on lower mountain slopes for timber. They also clear land to make space to keep farm animals such as sheep. To dig out useful minerals and coal, miners destroy large areas of mountain land. Power companies build power stations at the foot of mountain slopes. These use the force of stream or river water rushing downhill to spin special water wheels, which make electricity.

Science Behind It: Cutting down mountain forests

Trees on slopes hold the soil together and form a natural barrier that keeps mud and snow from sliding down. When mountain forests are cut down, there are more landslides and avalanches. Rainwater flows more quickly down mountain-sides, and can cause floods on land below the slopes.

These mountain slopes in Madagascar have been worn away because the trees were cut down.

Taking care of mountains

Conservation groups work to protect wild places. Some conservation groups care for mountains and hills. For example, they buy areas of land and pay people to look after it. They educate visitors about how to treat the land properly. Some conservation groups organize volunteers to help. They plant new trees to replace those that have been cut down, mend eroded paths and put up fences to stop farm animals straying into areas of rare plants. People like us can help these groups by donating money or volunteering your time.

Taking Action: Help our hills

There are lots of practical things you can do to help each time you visit hills or mountains. Stick to paths and mountain bike trails to avoid eroding land or crushing rare plants. Keep dogs on leads so they do not disturb any animals living there. Never drop litter as it may harm animals.

One way to help prevent mountain erosion is to plant trees. Their roots will hold the soil together.

How can we look after rivers and lakes?

Rivers and lakes are wild places that we like to visit to go swimming, fishing, boating, and for other enjoyable activities. We use the water they contain to drink, wash, and flush our toilets. Rivers and lakes are also home to fascinating plants and animals such as water lilies and rushes, frogs, fish, and dragonflies.

Yet people are spoiling rivers and lakes all over the world. They dump **polluting** waste such as litter and **sewage** into the water. Polluted water can harm wildlife. It is also more difficult to clean for our own use.

People also remove plants growing along the edges of rivers and lakes so they can get to the water more easily. This means that there is less shelter for animals such as ducks or otters to nest, and fewer shady patches where trout and salmon swim. With fewer plant roots to hold it together, the soil along the banks crumbles into the water and makes it dirty.

Animals such as this stork can be harmed by getting stuck in litter left in rivers and lakes by people.

Dirty water

When rain falls it washes pollution from the land into rivers. This polluted **run-off** includes petrol from roads, poisonous **leachate** from rubbish dumps and **fertilizers** from farmland. About four out of every ten rivers in the USA are too polluted for swimming or fishing.

Science Behind It: Blooming algae!

Tiny floating plants called algae that live in rivers and lakes need **nutrients** in the water to grow. Algae are part of many freshwater **food webs**. When water is polluted with fertilizer run-off it contains too many nutrients. This causes algae to bloom, which means they grow quickly and crowd the water. When the bloom dies, the algae sink to the bottom where **bacteria** rot them. Bacteria use up lots of **oxygen** from the water to help rot the algae. Then there is not enough oxygen left for animals such as fish to breathe, so they may die.

This stream is now lifeless following a bloom of algae.

Case Study: A cleaner stream

Children at Friends' Central Middle School in Pennsylvania, USA, are protecting their local stream from pollution. They have positioned logs, planted trees, and dug small ditches along the edges. These are all ways of slowing the run-off of polluted water from the street into the stream. The run-off soaks into the soil which filters out some of the pollution. The water that reaches the stream is then cleaner.

The more wildlife there is in and around water, the cleaner the water is likely to be!

Taking Action: Saving water

Here are some top tips for saving water at home:
- Turn off the tap as you brush your teeth.
- Take quick showers instead of baths. Showers use far less water to get you clean!
- Switch off lights and computers because river water is often used to make electricity.
- Catch the rainwater that falls on your house using rain butts (large containers). Use this rainwater, and not tap water, to wash your family's car or to water plants.

How can we keep coasts clean?

A coast is the place where land and sea meet. Coastlines are among the most beautiful and fragile **ecosystems** on our planet. From sandy beaches to rocky shores, coastal **habitats** shelter thousands of different kinds of fish, birds, sea turtles, and other marine animals. They also give people great pleasure when we go on holiday by the sea.

Bathers beware! The beaches that we play on and the sea that we swim in are being polluted by litter, sewage, and chemicals.

Coasts under threat

The major threats to coasts are **tourism** and **pollution**. People are clearing coasts to make room for holiday resorts and houses. But when people build new hotels, golf courses, or marinas they damage **coral reefs** and coastal forests, and concrete over stretches of coastal habitats. Coasts are polluted by litter, **sewage**, and other waste that is dumped in the sea. The waste carried by rivers as they flow out to sea also pollutes the coast.

Oil is one of the worst polluters of the coast. Ships can spill oil accidentally, or deliberately wash it into the sea. Oil floats and it traps animals at sea. The tides wash it ashore, where it harms coastal animals, seaweed, and ruins beaches. Jet skis are a new marine danger. These fast machines make a loud noise that chases timid coastal animals from their habitat. They also leak oil into the water.

Science Behind It: Oil and sea animals

A marine animal's fur or feathers trap air a bit like a wetsuit, keeping it warm and waterproof in the cold water. They do not work when coated with sticky oil, so animals may freeze to death. The weight of the oil may make the animal drown or prevent it getting away from **predators**. Marine animals are often poisoned or their insides damaged by the oil they eat. When they die, other animals eat them and are then poisoned too.

This seabird is struggling to survive after the coastline where it lives was polluted.

21

Case Study: Clean Beach Challenge

The Australian Clean Beach Challenge rewards young people and their families and communities for cleaning up the country's beaches. Moffat Beach, Queensland, was a prize-winning stretch of coast in 2003. The community has regular beach clean-ups to collect litter. They raised money to buy a probe for testing water quality. This helps them to spot any **pollution** problems quickly.

These people are taking part in a clean-up day at Sydney Harbour in Australia. Local people feel proud to help!

Taking Action: What can you do?

Never leave litter, and always take fishing hooks, lines, and nets home with you after you have been fishing. These can harm animals. If you go rock-pooling, always put stones back where you found them and never move animals from their homes. Don't buy souvenirs that are made from **endangered species** – such as coral or exotic shells – when you are on holiday.

Where are the habitats in towns and cities?

You might be surprised to know that thousands of **species** of plants and animals find places to live in towns and cities. They live in parks and tree-lined squares, gardens, playing fields, and churchyards. You will also find them in quiet, leafy banks alongside railway lines, rivers, and canals. Smaller plants and animals also make their homes under pavements, in walls, and even in our homes!

In cities, birds like this often nest on high buildings instead of on cliff ledges as they would in the countryside.

Changing places

Many animals move into towns and cities when their wild **habitats** are destroyed. Cities can be a good place to live. They are warm and sheltered, and for many animals there is plenty of food. Many creatures that can live in cities, such as rats, foxes, and pigeons, are **scavengers**. They live off leftover food that they find in bins or on the streets.

Problems for urban wildlife

Traffic is the biggest danger to city wildlife. Speeding vehicles kill many animals and exhaust fumes cause terrible air **pollution**. Waste and litter pollute ponds and parks, and sometimes people damage the trees that squirrels and other animals live in. When people use poisons to get rid of wildlife pests such as cockroaches and woodworm, they can accidentally harm other animals such as bees, spiders, and bats.

Gardens in towns and cities can be small or large, even high up on a roof. They provide a home for lots of animals, including insects, birds, bats, and squirrels.

Science Behind It: Predator and prey

Many wild **predators** are helpful to people because their **prey** are pests. Young ladybirds eat up the greenfly that destroy garden plants. A single little brown bat can catch and eat 600 mosquitoes in an hour! Spiders in our homes trap and eat the nuisance flies that can spoil our food.

City safari

Understanding where the wildlife is around us can help us care for it. Keep your eyes and ears open when you walk through city streets. Take time to look among tangled plant stems on a wall and you might see snails and small birds. Look down at the pavements and grass beneath your feet to see ants, earwigs, and grasshoppers. Pause by ponds to see insects such as pondskaters skimming the surface.

Taking Action: Helping urban wildlife

Here are some suggestions for looking after urban wildlife:

- Never drop litter or damage plants.
- Build a pile of leaves in the corner of your garden for animals such as toads and hedgehogs to **hibernate** in over winter.
- Put a bell on your cat, especially in spring, to warn baby birds and rodents that it is out hunting.
- Walk or cycle where and when you can to reduce the pollution caused by traffic.

You do not have to look far to find wildlife in a park or garden.

Is your school wildlife-friendly?

Your school playground might be the place where you and your friends run wild, but what about wildlife? There are often places around schools where animals live. Field mice or rabbits might live in the overgrown corner of a playing field. Birds may feed in a patch of trees or nest under the roof of a bike shed.

You can also attract more wildlife to your school by helping to create new **habitats**. Get together with your classmates and volunteer to make a school garden. Here you can grow plants such as buddleia or lilac that attract butterflies and moths. Carefully pile up logs in a corner. As they rot, they may form a home for important **decomposers** such as woodlice or toadstools.

Try growing plants in your school garden. They will attract insects such as caterpillars, and also birds that eat the caterpillars.

For the future

Once your wildlife garden is established, it will grow and develop and give pleasure to many schoolchildren even after you have grown up! If everyone on Earth were more responsible for the wild places surrounding them, then fewer animals and plants would become **extinct**. Caring for wild places makes sure there are unspoilt places for animals to live and for us to enjoy.

Attract wild birds to your school by putting out food or water. Keep your distance and watch how they behave!

Taking Action: Pond life

Why not make a shallow pond at school? Ask your teacher to help you dig a hole in the ground and line it with plastic to stop water escaping. Fill your pond with water from a local pond that should contain tiny plants and animals. Put in pondweed to add **oxygen** to the water. Ask local pond owners for fish or frogspawn to put in. Arrange rocks for frogs to climb in and out of the water. Plants around the edges will attract insects.

fact file

- There are now more than 500 million cars **polluting** the planet. Traffic fumes contain some of the most harmful substances known.
- Cleaning up pesticides in water in the UK costs over £200 million each year.
- In Australia, 41 mammal **species** have become **extinct** over the past 200 years. This is more than anywhere else on Earth. Another 117 are **endangered** and need to be protected.
- In the past 20 years, nearly 3000 square kilometres (700,000 acres) of wild **habitat** have been destroyed in California, USA.
- Each year over 5 million square kilometres (more than 2 million square miles) of forest are cut down around the world. That is an area over half the size of Australia!
- The area that is now called the Nouabale-Ndoki National Park in central Africa is such a remote, wild place that it has no trace of people ever having lived there.
- People live on, farm, fish, or mine over 80% of all the land surface of the Earth.
- Antarctica is a huge continent – it is 14 million square kilometres – but has no permanent human population.

find out more

Books to read

Science Answers: Food Chains and Webs, Richard and Louise Spilsbury (Heinemann Library, 2004)

Taking Action: Friends of the Earth, Louise Spilsbury (Heinemann Library, 2000)

Taking Action: WWF, Louise Spilsbury (Heinemann Library, 2000)

Websites

There are many useful websites to help you learn more and make plans for taking action of your own.

Friends of the Earth – the website of this major international organization has lots of information about projects and campaigns:
www.foei.org

WWF – another large organization which has lots of information on its website:
www.wwf.org

Greenpeace – a large international environmental organization:
www.greenpeace.org

The British Trust for Conservation Volunteers – gives ideas how you can get involved in helping wild places:
www.btcv.org

London Zoo – one of the world's major zoos and a leader in global conservation:
www.londonzoo.co.uk

Earth Sanctuaries – learn about the work of Earth Sanctuaries in Australia:
www.esl.com.au

Glossary

adapt when a living thing has special features that help it survive in its particular habitat

bacteria tiny living things that live in air, water, or soil

conservation taking action to protect plants, animals, and wild habitats

coral reef underwater structure formed of coral, a hard substance made by living things called polyps

decomposer living thing that breaks down dead organisms, such as plants and animals

ecosystem habitat and all the different living things that live there together make an ecosytem

endangered species plant or animal in danger of becoming extinct

environmental to do with the environment – the surroundings in which we and other living things live

extinct describes a plant or animal species that has died out

fertilizer chemical that helps plants grow

food web diagram that shows the order in which food energy is passed from plants to animals

habitat natural home of a group of plants and animals

hibernate when animals go into a special kind of deep sleep to avoid the bad weather and lack of food in winter

leachate black liquid that forms as waste rots

nutrient chemical that plants and animals need to live

oxygen one of the gases in the air that animals need to breathe to stay alive

pollen grains made by plants in flowers. Male cells in pollen from one flower join with female cells from another to produce seeds.

pollution something that makes air, water, or other parts of the Earth's environment dirty

predator animal that catches and eats other animals

prey animal that is caught and eaten by other animals

recycle collect things made from a material that can be broken down and remade into new things, such as newspapers, plastic or glass bottles

run-off rainwater that drains into rivers from the land

scavenger animal that eats dead animals or waste it finds, instead of catching its own food

sewage human bodily waste carried away from homes and other buildings in sewer pipes

species group of living things that are very similar. Males and females of the same species can breed to produce healthy offspring.

tourism industry that organizes holidays and holiday activities and services for people

Index